Riverside Studios, The Culture Project, Jane Bergere,
Dede Harris, Ruth Hendel, Mort Swinsky, Cheryl Wiensfield present

D0716042

The Exonerated

by Jessica Blank and Erik Jensen

First performed at 45 Bleecker Street, New York,
10 October 2002

The London season opened at Riverside Studios on
21 February 2006

www.theexonerated.co.uk

The Exonerated

The play was developed in Los Angeles by the Actors' Gang, in association with The Culture Project in 2002, and opened later the same year at 45 Bleecker St in New York City.

The play concluded its full production run in March 2004, after running for a year and a half at 45 Bleecker St. It also toured the USA stopping in Philadelphia, New Orleans, San Francisco, Fort Worth and Minneapolis, amongst others, and featured performances from Robin Williams, Brian Dennehy, Mia Farrow, Stockard Channing, and many more.

The play's UK debut was at the Edinburgh Festival Fringe 2005, produced by Assembly Theatre in association with The Culture Project and Marshall Cordell, and the same production opened in London at the Riverside Studios in February 2006.

Winner Fringe First Award
Edinburgh 2005

Winner Herald Angel Award
Edinburgh 2005

Winner Champion of Justice Award
National Association of Criminal Defense Lawyers 2005

Winner Freedom of Expression Award
Amnesty International 2005

Winner Drama Desk Award
for Unique Theatrical Experience 2003

Winner Outer Critics Circle Award
for Outstanding Off-Broadway Play 2003

Winner Lucille Lortel Award
for Unique Theatrical Experience 2003

L.A. Ovation Award
for Best World Premiere Play 2002

Over the summer of 2000 we travelled across the United States and sat in people's living rooms as they related to us the most amazing stories we had ever heard. All of those we interviewed (40 on the phone, and from those initial contacts, 20 in person) had been sentenced to death, spent anywhere from 2 to 22 years on death row and were subsequently found innocent and freed by the State. These interviews form the core of *The Exonerated*. We also spent countless hours in the dusty record rooms of state courthouses, poured through thousands of microfiche files and cardboard boxes full of affidavits, depositions, police interrogations and court transcripts in order to fill in the story gaps. We pulled quotes from newspapers, TV footage and magazines.

We want to stress that with a few exceptions, each word spoken in the play came from public record: 'found' legal documents, a transcript, a letter or an article about the case. For staging purposes we condensed, added, theatricalised, combined and extrapolated dramatic/comedic moments for the presentation. But the vast majority of the piece is as it was said by the actual participants.

We are not responsible for the content of the public record or of the interviews in any way, except to report what was said to us by the exonerated. That said, none of these interviews, transcripts or the play itself should be considered completely representative of these cases. A full transcript of a trial can be somewhere in the realm of 50 to 60 thousand pages. With only 90 minutes to relate the events of these lives there are bound to be differences of opinion, omission of details and technical legal matters which cannot be fully represented.

It is our intention to relate as fully as possible what it is like to be wrongly accused and convicted, what it is like to be on death row, and what it is like to get out and be in the world again. This is not primarily a play about anger and revenge (although these feelings do come into play). It is really a play about strength, hope, redemption, and forgiveness.

Jessica Blank and Erik Jensen

On May 20th this year, it will be 19 years since my client Edward Earl Johnson was gassed to death in Mississippi for a crime he didn't commit. The last two weeks of his life were filmed for the documentary *Fourteen Days in May*, which demonstrated the reality of the death penalty to people in Britain, and inspired hundreds to volunteer their time working on behalf of people on death row. From that sad seed the UK charity *Reprieve* was grown, and is now fighting for the lives of people facing the death penalty around the world.

Tonight you will hear the stories of six innocent survivors of death row. Edward's story cannot be among them as he did not survive to be exonerated, despite compelling evidence of his innocence. These six stories represent just the tip of the iceberg. 122 people have been exonerated from death row since 1973 in the USA alone.

The risk of executing the innocent will eventually bring about the end of capital punishment. This production is doing its part, bringing audiences face to face with the intolerable human consequences of wrongful conviction. I just wish Edward could be here to have a role in it.

Clive Stafford Smith, Legal Director, Reprieve
(www.reprieve.org.uk)

The Exonerated

Performed by a revolving cast, changing
weekly. Theatregoers will find this
performance's cast details on the sheet
provided. For full details of the London cast
go to www.theexonerated.co.uk

written by	Jessica Blank and Erik Jensen
directed by	Bob Balaban
casting director	Stephen Moore
company manager	Tom Jeffords
technical manager	Barbra Egervary
marketing manager	Sarah Mallett
production assistants	Alex Bowley
	Elizabeth Brown
press representation	Borkowski PR (020 7404 3000)
graphic design	www.snowcreative.co.uk
advertising	aka, www.akauk.com
producer	Louise Chantal
executive producers	Allan Buchman
	William Burdett-Coutts
other partners	Amnesty, Reprieve, Human Rights Watch, Human Rights Lawyers' Association, Centre for Crime and Justice Studies at Kings College London, Redress, Human Writes, and the Prison Reform Trust.
thanks to	John Buzetti, James Caygill, Claudia Courtis, Fiona Duff, Huw Jenkins, Geraint Lewis, James Seabright, Kate Treglown, Dinah Wood at Faber & Faber, and everyone at Riverside Studios.

The Authors

Jessica Blank and **Erik Jensen** are actors and writers. Together they are authors of *The Exonerated*, which has won several awards and been made into a television movie for Court TV starring Susan Sarandon, Danny Glover, Brian Dennehy, Aidan Quinn and Delroy Lindo. Their book on the making of The Exonerated, *Living Justice*, was published in 2005 by Simon and Schuster.

As an actor **Jessica Blank** has appeared on television in *Law and Order: Criminal Intent*, *Rescue Me*, *One Life to Live*, and *Guiding Light*; film credits include *The Namesake* (dir. Mira Nair), *Undermind*, and *The Exonerated* (for Court TV). She has acted in theatres throughout New York City.

Erik Jensen has co-starred in over a dozen feature films, including 20th Century Fox's *Black Knight* and Dreamworks' *The Love Letter*. He has appeared on television regularly on CBS' *Love Monkey* and CSI, and NBC's *Deadline*, as well as *Alias*, *Law and Order*, and *Century City*, amongst others. He recently co-starred in the TNT pilot *The Dark* (dir. Walter Hill, prod. Stephen Cannell) with Fred Ward. Notable stage appearances include Arthur Kopit's *Y2K* directed by Bob Balaban and Terrence McNally's *Corpus Christi* at Manhattan Theatre Club.

The Company

Bob Balaban – *Director*
Bob directed and produced the original off-Broadway production of *The Exonerated*, as well as the television version for Court TV. He has just finished directing and producing a movie about the life of Doris Duke, starring Susan Sarandon and Ralph Fiennes. Other directing credits include *The Last Good Time* and *Parents*. He produced and co-starred in the award winning film *Gosford Park*. His acting career spans more than fifty films including *Capote, A Mighty Wind, Ghost World, The Mexican, Best in Show, Cradle Will Rock, Waiting for Guffman, Absence of Malice, Prince of the City, Close Encounters of the Third Kind, Catch-22* and *Midnight Cowboy*, as well as M. Night Shyamalan's latest, *Lady in the Water* and Christopher Guest's *For Your Consideration*, both coming soon. His New York theatre appearances include *Plaza Suite, The Inspector General* (Tony Award nomination*), Speed the Plow, You're a Good Man Charlie Brown, Marie and Bruce* and *Some Americans Abroad*. He is also author of *McGrowl*, a best-selling series of children's books.

Stephen Moore – *Casting Director*
Stephen was Assistant Casting Director on the feature films *Starter for Ten, Amazing Grace, The Good Night, The Illusionist, Sahara, Imagine Me & You, Brothers of the Head* and *I Capture the Castle*; and television dramas including *Rome, Longford, The Virgin Queen, He Knew He Was Right, Byron, Final Demand* and *The Inspector Linley Mysteries*. He worked as Casting Director on *Perpetua* (Latchmere Theatre), the short film *Chicken Soup* and the Rocliffe New Writing Forums.

Tom Jeffords – *Company Manager*
Tom is thrilled to continue his involvement with *The Exonerated* after serving as the show's Stage Manager in New York. He has worked on tours including: *The Boy Friend, A Funny Thing Happened…, VeggieTales Live!, Jesus Christ Superstar, Macbeth* (a co-production by the NEA and the US Dept. of Defense). Other credits include: De La Guarda's *Villa Villa* (in New York and Seoul) and *It's Karate Kid, The Musical*.

the cultureproject

The Culture Project is one of New York's most prominent off-Broadway theatre companies with an abiding commitment to presenting dramatic works that explore today's defining social and political issues. It views the performing arts as a critical national resource. Our purpose is to address injustice, embrace diversity and effect social change. The Culture Project has established an artistic ideal providing a creative home to a diverse array of artists who share its passion for amplifying the voices of the disenfranchised, disaffected and politically marginalized.

The company was propelled into national prominence by the original production of *The Exonerated*. On the heels of this success The Culture Project and Meryl Streep co-produced *Bridge and Tunnel*. With *Guantánamo: Honor Bound to Defend Freedom*, The Culture Project shone a bright and dramatic light on the atrocities perpetrated in the Guantánamo prison camp in the name of freedom. In *Belfast Blues*, the company probed the human dimensions of political violence through the story of the "troubles" in Ireland. These productions and others have garnered a generous array of Drama Desk, OBIE, and Outer Circle Critics awards, among many others. This recognition reignites The Culture Project's passion for its goal and reinforces its commitment to hard-hitting and provocative theatre as a powerful ingredient in shaping our nation's values debate.

Heading into its second decade, The Culture Project is currently presenting *RFK*, a new play about Robert F. Kennedy and his fight for civil rights and the democratic inclusiveness of the American Dream. Next, The Culture Project will present *Guardians*, a story about the United States army and the UK press – the twin scandals of the war in Iraq and the eerie collision of America and Britain. In September, The Culture Project will launch an annual multi-disciplinary, multi-venue festival focused on issue-based art.

www.45bleecker.com

RIVERSIDESTUDIOS

Riverside Studios is a unique arts and media centre on the banks of the Thames in Hammersmith, comprising performance studios, a cinema, a television studio and production gallery, rehearsal/workshop space, numerous offices and a large contemporary cafe/bar and river terrace. As well as being one of the original homes of the BBC, the studios became famous throughout the 1970's and 1980's for bringing some of the most exciting international theatre work to the UK.

The BBC gave up the studios in the early 70s but prior to this, the building saw the creation of many classics, *Dr Who*, *Terry and June*, *Hancock's Half Hour*, *Z Cars* and *Quatermass*, to name a few. It's more recent television history began with *TFI Friday* and has since seen hosts of productions from *Rory Bremner* to *CD-UK*.

The TV world in this context has rubbed shoulders with a host of live performance wonders from Dario Fo to Peter Brook, Robert Lepage, Theatre de Complicite to Cheek by Jowl.

The studios started life as an iron foundry building water pumps and corrugated iron for the colonies. The First World War saw it turn into a munitions factory and shortly after this it became a film studio, the most famous production made here being *The Seventh Vale*. Today, film is celebrated through a highly respected programme of international film.

Riverside's vision is founded on respecting its unique historical foundations whilst forging a new and dynamic centre for live performance, cinema, television and education. Our aspiration is to present theatre work that is 'epic' and international in quality, whilst continuing to support and showcase new and up-and-coming companies.

www.riversidestudios.co.uk

Amnesty International opposes the death penalty in all cases. We believe that capital punishment is wrong in principle. It is also violent, cruel, often racist, arbitrary and political, and it is frequently used against the poor, political opponents, the badly represented, racial minorities and the mentally ill. It should have no place in a modern criminal justice system.

Capital punishment is not an effective deterrent and due to its irrevocable nature, does not allow for mistakes and miscarriages of justice to be rectified. Currently over half the world's countries have abolished the death penalty in law or practice. Of these, 86 countries have abolished the death penalty for all crimes, 11 have abolished it for all but exceptional crimes (war crimes etc.) and 25 countries have abolished the practice of execution (though it remains on the statute books).

A particular case of concern to Amnesty International is Kenny Richey, a Scot who has been on death row in Ohio since 1987. He has always protested his innocence, refusing to take a plea bargain that would have resulted in a lesser sentence. He has had 13 separate execution dates and continues to fight to have fresh evidence heard in a US court.

For more information on Amnesty International and the death penalty, see www.amnesty.org.uk/deathpenalty

Reprieve is a charity that fights for the lives of people facing the death penalty and other human rights violations. Founded in 1999 by lawyer Clive Stafford Smith, Reprieve focuses on the cases of the innocent, people who are mentally ill or learning disabled, women, racial and ethnic minorities, and those detained out of reach of the law in the 'war on terror'.

Through investigations, legal representation, campaigns and education, we target issues and cases where we can make a difference. We fight for those who cannot afford a lawyer to defend them. And we fight to change the legal systems that - casually and systematically - allow fatal miscarriages of justice.

To find out what you can do to help Reprieve exonerate prisoners on death row, please visit our website: www.reprieve.org.uk.

Reprieve is a registered charity (1080147)

Riverside Studios

Jessica Blank and Erik Jensen

The Exonerated

faber and faber

First published in the USA in 2004 by Faber and Faber Inc.,
an affiliate of Farrar, Straus and Giroux LLC, New York

First published in the UK in 2006
by Faber and Faber Limited
3 Queen Square, London WC1N 3AU

Typeset by Country Setting, Kingsdown, Kent CT14 8ES
Printed in England by Mackays of Chatham plc, Chatham, Kent

A CIP record for this book is available from the British Library

ISBN 0–571–23366–X
978–0–571–23366–3

2 4 6 8 10 9 7 5 3 1

For the exonerated
and for those who are still waiting

Acknowledgements

The Exonerated would not have been created without the generous and selfless support of countless people. First and foremost, we would like to thank the exonerated individuals who told us their stories. Their courage is a gift to all of us. We are also grateful to The Actors' Gang, Chris Ajemian, Shawn Armbrust, the Artists Network, Kara Baker, Bob Balaban, Eve Battaglia, Jordan Berlant, the Blank family, the Boehm Foundation, Carolyn Bowles and Craig Roth, Larry Breakstone and Karen Levy, Julie Brimberg, Richmond and Sandy Browne, Allan Buchman, John Buzzetti, Gabriel Byrne, the Center on Wrongful Convictions, the Culture Project, Mindy Duitz and the George Soros Foundation, Bonnie Cottle, Glenn Daniels, Micki Dickoff, Wendy Eaton, Robert Edgar, Ginny and Terry Eicher, David Elliott, Curtis Ellis, Cyrena Esposito, Mike Farrell, Barbara and Richard Feldman, the Fortune Society, The Funding Exchange, Leslie Garis, Thom Gates, the Gersh Agency, Lynne Godwin, Nancy and Lou Goodman, Andrew and Jane Gordon, Alan Grabelsky, Colin Greer and the New World Foundation, Samuel Gross, Nick Hallett, Carolyn Halliday and CR Schult, Enid Harlow, Gail Hartman, Jason Helm, Ginny Hepler, Barbara Heyer, Neal and Clara Hulkower, the Innocence Project, Richard Jaffe, the Jensen family, Anna and Michael Johnson-Chase, Connie Julian, the Justice Project, Casey Kait, Cathy Kanner and Kanner Entertainment, Jessica Kaplan and Steve Symonds, Moises Kaufman, Jen Knestrick, Arthur Kopit, Nancy and Jerry Kobrin, the Ethel and Abe Lapides Foundation, Darrell Larson, Gerry Lefcourt, Diana Levy and Bruce Fabens, Arthur

Lewis, Roz Lichter, Joe Mantello, Maria Markosov,
Larry Marshall, the Mattis family, Jim McCloskey
and Centurion Ministries, Marghe Mills-Thysen,
Kim Moarefi, Peter Neufeld, the New York State Council
for the Arts, Paul Nugent, Nellie Nugiel, Arlene Popkin,
Nina Pratt, Andrew Price, Greg Reiner, Speedy Rice,
Riptide Communications, David Robbins, Tim Robbins,
Mordechai Rochlin, Steve Rothstein, Allan Rowand,
Joshua Rubenstein, Diann Rust-Tierney, Susan Sarandon,
Kate Schumaecker, Elizabeth Semel, Olivia Mellon
Shapiro, Robert and Elizabeth Sheehan, Alison Shigo,
Anne Smith, Kent Spriggs, Barry Scheck, Edward Steele,
Ronald Tabak, Yasuko Takahara, Zoe Tanabaum,
Robert Warden, Helen Whitney, Sarah Whitson and
Josh Zinner, the crews of the Los Angeles and New York
productions, the New York City producing team, and
all the extraordinary actors who have workshopped or
appeared in *The Exonerated*. It would not have been
possible without you.

Introduction

Over the summer of 2000, we traveled across the United States, sat in people's living rooms, and listened as they told us what it was like to be innocent and on death row. They were from vastly different ethnic, religious, and educational backgrounds. Their views on the world varied greatly. The only thing they held in common was that they had each been sentenced to die, spent anywhere from two to twenty-two years on death row, and had been freed amidst overwhelming evidence of their innocence. We interviewed forty people on the phone and twenty in person. Six of these interviews form the core of *The Exonerated*.

The previous spring, we had gotten the idea for the play at a conference on the death penalty at Columbia University. We took the idea to producer Allan Buchman, a friend of ours from the downtown theater community in New York who ran the Culture Project.

Governor George Ryan of Illinois had just declared a moratorium on the death penalty in his state, and another George was running for high office – with more executions carried out under his watch as governor of Texas than in any other state since the reinstatement of the death penalty in 1976. The issue was very much in the news. Allan told us we could have his theater for three nights in the fall if we could have something up before the elections. So we hit the road. We went as far north and west as Chicago, as far south as Texas and Miami, and just about everywhere in between to meet the people whose stories appear in this play.

We returned from the interviews with hours and hours of tape, which became several hundred pages of transcripts. We're both primarily actors, which means we have lots of talented and underemployed friends. We enlisted them to come workshop the transcripts with us, and began the process of shaping thousands of pages of everyday speech into a play. At the same time, we called director Bob Balaban and asked him to direct three readings of the play at Allan's theater that fall. Bob brought his highly trained eye to the material we were developing, while also helping us assemble a cast for the readings. That cast included Gabriel Byrne, Ossie Davis, Vincent D'Onofrio, Charles Dutton, Cherry Jones, David Morse, Susan Sarandon, Tim Robbins, Debra Winger, and many other extraordinary actors. They performed an initial version of the play, which then consisted of the stories of twelve exonerated people, taken entirely from the interviews we had conducted.

After three readings at the Culture Project and a performance at the United Nations, we hit the road again. It was clear to us, Bob, and our audiences how the exonerated people felt about what had happened to them; what was still unclear was how it could've happened in the first place. So we went through the extremely difficult process of paring down the number of stories in the play in order to tell each one more fully. Additionally, we dug into the court transcripts and case files of the people whose stories we were telling. We spent countless hours in dusty courthouse record rooms, pawing through thousands of microfiche files and cardboard boxes full of affidavits, depositions, police interrogations, and courtroom testimony. The court employees assumed we were law students – and we did nothing to discourage that belief. With a few exceptions, each word spoken in this play comes from the public record – legal documents, court transcripts, letters – or from an interview with an exonerated person. The names of the exonerated people are their own; some names of auxiliary characters have been fictionalized for legal reasons.

The vast majority of the piece is as it was said, two, five, ten, and twenty years ago by the actual participants. At the time we conducted these interviews, there were eighty-nine people who had been exonerated from death row. As of this writing, there are now 122. We consider every one of their stories to be part of this play.

Notes on the American Productions

The first full production of *The Exonerated* was at the Actors' Gang in Los Angeles. Six months later, it opened Off-Broadway at the 45 Bleecker Theater. The Actors' Gang production was fully staged, with entrances, exits, a scrim, and simple set pieces; Bob Balaban's Off-Broadway production was performed by ten actors seated in chairs for the duration of the play, with all environments and scene changes defined by lights and sound. Both ways of presenting the play worked, not least because both were minimal and unfussy, with the focus on the stories and on the actors who were telling them. This is a good rule of thumb for directors staging *The Exonerated*. It works either fully staged or with seated actors in a 'story theater' format as long as both the staging and storytelling are kept very simple.

Directors and actors should be careful not to be didactic in their presentation of the play. The drama of these stories does not need enhancement: It's generally a good idea to avoid stapling newspaper headlines to the back wall or throwing electric chairs all over the stage. Similarly, actors playing exonerated people should avoid overemotionalizing. These characters have been exonerated for a number of years. They have, of course, been deeply affected by their experiences in varying ways, all of which are integral to the play – but, except for a few instances, they are *telling* their stories, not *reliving* them. Trust the stories.

Also, all should keep in mind that because of the subject matter, things can get overly dark rather quickly. There are undeniably dramatic moments in the play – but remember that these are six stories of people who *survived*. There's a great deal of humor here, too – don't overlook it.

There are ten actors. Six play one exonerated person each; two play wives of the exonerated; and two male ensemble actors play the supporting cast of characters. Ensemble actors should establish a strong and clear personality for each character they play. They should also pay attention to the geographical location of each of the stories they appear in, keep the dialects specific, and be careful not to get generic southern for everything; it's an easy trap to fall into here. Ensemble actors should also take care not to tip into caricature in their portrayal of the authorities. These characters all have a job to do, and are generally convinced their actions are justified and right.

All the actors, with the *possible* exception of the actor playing David, should take care to find the humor in their characters. It's pretty difficult to make it through an experience this harrowing without the ability to laugh sometimes. Too much gravity and depression bring the play down; the actor playing Delbert should be especially careful about this. Delbert has an extraordinary sense of humor about himself and the world; to play only his gravitas is to do him a disservice.

Because the death penalty itself is inextricably connected to race, it is important that white people play white people and black people play black people. We strongly support nontraditional casting in general; but in the case of this play, it dilutes the reality of many of the issues involved.

Finally, we ask that any actors and directors working on this play respect the exonerated people's privacy by refraining from contacting them directly. Research is important, but these individuals' privacy and comfort are more so. Besides, in the process of watching more than one hundred actors work on these roles, we've found that actors usually do better when they don't meet the real people and/or watch videotapes of them during the rehearsal process. Over and over, we've seen completely disparate actors, after spending some time with these words, unintentionally begin to channel the people they are playing, down to their speech patterns and mannerisms. It happens involuntarily and has nothing to do with mimicry or impersonation.

It's all in the words, and in the stories.

The Exonerated was originally presented in Los Angeles by the Actor's Gang (Tim Robbins, artistic director), in association with the Culture Project, on 19 April 2002. The cast was as follows:

Kerry Ken Palmer
Sunny Adele Robbins
Delbert Richard Lawson
Robert Ken Elliott
David Ben Cain
Gary Brian Powell
Female Ensemble 1 Yolanda Snowball
Female Ensemble 2 Victoria Cunningham
Female Ensemble 3 Blaire Chandler
Male Ensemble 1 Kelly Cole
Male Ensemble 2 Jon Kellam
Male Ensemble 3 Terrell Tilford

Directed by Jessica Blank and Erik Jensen
Supervising direction by Bob Balaban
Set designed by Richard Hoover
Costumes designed by Ann Closs-Farley
Lghting by Ellen Monocroussos
Sound by David Robbins
Production Stage Manager Leah Harrison

The Exonerated premiered in New York City on 10 October 2002 at 45 Bleecker, produced by the Culture Project in association with Patrick Blake and David Elliott. The cast was as follows:

Kerry Richard Dreyfuss
Sunny Jill Clayburgh
Delbert Charles Brown
Robert David Brown, Jr
David Curtis McClarin
Gary Jay O. Sanders
Female Ensemble 1 April Yvette Thompson
Female Ensemble 2 Sara Gilbert
Male Ensemble 1 Bruce Kronenberg
Male Ensemble 2 Phil Levy

Directed by Bob Balaban
Set designed by Tom Ontiveros
Costumes designed by Sara J. Tosetti
Music and Sound by David Robbins
Production Stage Manager Thomas J. Gates

Doubling

Male Ensemble 1 plays White Cop 1, Kerry's Defense,
Sheriff Carroll, Jesse, Court Attorney, David's Prosecutor,
Inmate, White Guard, Jeff, Cellmate, Ex-Boyfriend
and Farmer.

Male Ensemble 2 plays White Cop 2, Kerry's Prosecutor,
Rhodes, Deputy, Southern White Guy, Robert's Judge,
David's Defense, Doyle and Robert's Prosecutor.

Female Ensemble 1 (Georgia) also plays
State Attorney, Kerry's Judge, and Darla.

Female Ensemble 2 (Sandra /Sue) also plays
Female Lawyer.

The roles of Black Cop, Black Guy 1 and Black Inmate
are played by the actor who plays David.

The role of Black Guy 2 is played by the actor
who plays Robert.

Characters

Delbert
African-American, sixty. A seminary dropout, radical,
and poet. His whole personality is like an old soul song:
smooth, mellow, and with an underlying rhythm
that never lets up. Actors playing Delbert should
take care to find his substantial sense of humor,
in addition to his obvious depth.

Sunny
White, fifty. A bright, pixieish yoga teacher
from California; her lightness and positivity contrast
with moments of great depth and clarity.

Robert
African-American, thirties. A former horse groomer
from the Deep South; hardened but not lacking
a sense of humor. Deep rural Mississippi accent.

Georgia / Female Ensemble 1
African-American, thirty. Robert's wife, also southern;
extremely outspoken and warm. She and Robert
have a lovingly contentious relationship.
Loves to speak her mind.

Gary
White, forty-five. A midwestern hippie and an organic
farmer. Clearly was in his element in the late 1960s
and early 1970s. He is generally good-natured,
friendly, and quite smart.

Kerry
White, forty-five. A nineteen-year-old trapped
in a forty-five-year-old's body, born and bred in Texas.

Kerry was imprisoned for twenty-two of his
forty-five years and is eager to rediscover the world.
Always wants to make sure he connects with
whomever he is talking to. Strong Texas accent.

David
African-American, forty. A gentle, sad man,
born and raised in northern Florida (otherwise known
as southern Alabama). Has a very strong spiritual sense
and had aspirations to the ministry before being put on
death row at eighteen. He is continually engaged in
a battle between resignation and hope.

Sandra / Sue / Female Ensemble 2
White, forty. Sandra is married to Kerry.
Sweet, nurturing, loves Kerry dearly and has
a great sense of humor about him. She has
a strong Texas accent. Sue is married to Gary.
Salt of the earth; she is also an organic farmer.
She has a *strong* upper-Midwest accent – think *Fargo*.

Male Ensemble 1 and 2
Both white, thirty-five to fifty. Male Ensemble 1 and 2
play police officers, attorneys, suspects, and other
supporting characters. Both actors should be good
with dialects and characterization, and different from
each other in build and appearance. Both roles
require highly versatile, commanding actors.

THE EXONERATED

*Open on a stage bare except for ten plain armless chairs.
These chairs can be used variously to set up scenes
throughout the piece. The entire play can be performed
using only these chairs. No further set pieces are necessary,
although tables and other set pieces might work, too.
The play is seamless: there are no blackouts during the
performance, and no intermission. Unless otherwise
noted, the exonerated people deliver their monologues to
the audience. Delbert can see the other exonerated people;
unless otherwise noted, none of the other exonerated
people see one another or Delbert. At various points in
the play, we see 'scenes' illustrating the stories being told
by the exonerated. These scenes exist in the exonerated
people's memories, and unless otherwise noted, they
should take place behind or beside the character telling
the story.*

*Delbert functions as a sort of Chorus, fading in and
out of the action. He is a black man, sixty. His whole
personality is like an old soul song: smooth, mellow, but
with a relentless underlying rhythm. He has a great sense
of humor. He's from Chicago.*

Delbert This is not the place for thought that does not
    end in concreteness;
  it is not easy to be open or too curious.
  It is dangerous to dwell too much on things:
  to wonder who or why or when, to wonder how, is
    dangerous.
  How do we, the people, get outta this hole, what's the
    way to fight,

might I do what Richard and Ralph and Langston
'n them did?
It is not easy to be a poet here. Yet I sing.
I sing.

*Lights up on Sue and Gary. Sue is Gary's wife. Farmer
woman, salt of the earth. She has a very strong upper-
Midwest accent – think* Fargo.
*Gary is a midwestern hippie in his mid-forties. He is
an organic farmer. He was clearly in his element in the
late 1960s and early 1970s. He is generally good-
natured and quite smart.*

Gary Gary Gauger. This is my wife, Sue.

Beat. Sue waves.

So my case – the day before, I had gone to work here;
you see our workshop is a little building right over there.
And it is about ninety-two per cent recycled.

Sue Even the shingles and the foundation are recycled.

Gary So anyway, I start my plants out there, and then in
mid-March we move 'em out front to the hotbeds. So
I would come over here in the morning and work all day,
and I'd go back for supper at night.
So anyways, that day, I went to work; my folks
weren't around.

Sue But they had been planning a trip to Sugar Grove.

Gary I just thought, 'No big deal, they go away sometimes.'
By night, they didn't get home, I was worried about 'em.
I said, 'Jeez, they must've gotten in a car accident.' But
what do you do, call hospitals?

Sue Oh, ya can't. Ya can't. Not between here and Sugar
Grove.

Gary And the police, I knew, wouldn't investigate until they'd been missing for twenty-four hours. So I just basically stayed by the phone till midnight, went to bed.

Next morning, I got up to call the police, and a customer came walkin' up the driveway, looking for motorcycle parts, and in the back room, where we thought the part might be, is where we found my father's body.

Now, it looked to me like he'd suffered a stroke, because he was facedown in a pool of blood. And he obviously . . . was dead. I felt his pulse.

So, all of a sudden, here's my father's body; my mom's been missing. So I called the paramedics, who called the police, who told me they suspected foul play.

About an hour and a half later, they find my mother's body in a trailer out in front of the house. She had been killed and covered with rugs and pillows. (*Pause.*) They had been hidden, and their throats were slashed.

Two and a half hours after I found my parents, they had me arrested.

Lights down on Gary and Sue, up on Delbert.

Delbert It is not easy:
  you stand waiting for a train
  or a bus that may never come
  no friend drives by to catch a ride
  cold, tired:
  call yourself a poet
  but work all day mopping floors and looking out
    for thieves . . .

Lights down on Delbert, up on Robert and his wife, Georgia. Robert is a black man in his mid-thirties, hardened but not lacking a sense of humor, with a deep rural Mississippi accent. Georgia is also southern; outspoken, earthy, contentious, and extremely warm. Loves to speak her mind. The two of them overlap,

*finish each other's sentences, and otherwise play off
each other whenever they appear together.*

Robert Robert Earl Hayes. This here's my wife –

Georgia Georgia Hayes.

Robert (*sotto voce*) Baby, they know your last name –

Georgia I know; I just wanted to introduce myself. Go
ahead.

Robert Now, at the time that all this happened, I was
working around the racetrack, takin' care of the horses
you know. And at that racetrack, this white girl, she gets
raped and killed. And you know, she be dating the black
guys, and when she got killed, they ask me have I ever
had sex with the girl. I told them yeah, they said –

White Cop 1 Well, were you having sex with her that
night?

Robert I said no. Then they said –

White Cop 1 Well, why does she like hanging out on the
black side of the track?

Robert So I said, 'I don't know why she like hanging out
back there, I guess we more fun.'
   But this girl, she got killed. And the cop came to my
job the next morning, they said –

White Cop 1 We gotta talk to you.

Robert I said okay, I went to the police station. And they
kept saying –

White Cop 2 We know what happened –

White Cop 1 We know you asked her for a date, and she
hit you –

White Cop 2 – and you hit her back –

White Cop 1 – and you didn't *mean* to hit her that hard.

Lights down on Cops.

Robert They just came right after me. This white girl, me and she had dated, and you know people round here don't like that too much. An' in my first trial, I *knew* I was going to prison – I had eleven whites and one black on that jury.

Georgia And do you think, seriously – now be honest – if the roles had been reversed, if it had been a black woman and a white man, it woulda been like that?

Robert Right, 'cause let's go to another high-profile case.

Georgia Oh, here we go –

Robert Now within all y'all's hearts – now be honest – within your *heart*, do you really think O.J. committed that crime?

Georgia (*laughing*) Well, but O.J., you know, I'm black and I *still* think he guilty, I'm sorry – I don't care what they say; I say, if the DNA put you there, O.J., you guilty.

Lights down on Robert and Georgia, up on Kerry and Sandra. Kerry is an eager nineteen-year-old trapped in a forty-five-year-old's body, white, with a Texas accent. Kerry is an 'up-talker' – he ends many of his sentences with a question mark. Sandra is Kerry's wife, also Texan, very pregnant, very sweet, takes care of Kerry.

Kerry Kerry Max Cook. (*Beat.*)

Sandra Sandra Cook.

Kerry It actually started when I was in the ninth or tenth grade. Me and my friends would, you know, act like we were going to school and then run out the back door and start trying to find a car with the keys in it. And I had the misfortune that one of the cars that I stole, in my adventures to conquer the world, was the sheriff deputy's car and I, ah . . . wrecked it – driver's ed I didn't take – and, make a long story short, the deputy beat me for it.

And that was pretty much it – after that, any robbery, any broken window, any cat up a tree, everything was just *my fault*, as far as the sheriff was concerned.

And then, fast-forwarding, I'm nineteen, and I'm at this apartment complex in Tyler, Texas, called the Embarcadero – there's a swimming pool there; it's where all the hip people hang out. And I was an attractive guy; I dressed real nice. It was the seventies you know, man: I bought my clothes from the hippest place, like the Gap, and I had my hair styled real long, platform shoes and bell-bottoms. I looked tight. And I was walkin' towards the swimming pool, and there was this beautiful gorgeous girl, man.

(*to Sandra*) Not as pretty as you.

Sandra Go on.

Kerry But really *gorgeous*, man – just nude and fondling herself, right there in the window. So I look up and I go, 'Oh my God, man . . . wow.' 'Cause I had lived a very sheltered, naive life, I'd never even been to a strip club before – and I'm seeing this total complete mature woman, and I'm goin', 'Okay, yeah, that's cool, man.'

And so anyway, a couple days go by, and I'm back at the pool and there's this chick layin' out there. To make a long story short, we started talking, told her I was a bartender in Dallas – course I was working at a gay bar, but I didn't tell her that – I'm just stretching everything as much as I can because I want to be all that plus a bag of potater chips. Anyway, we end up going back to her apartment . . . We . . . uh . . . you know . . . made out.

Sandra (*to audience*) But not . . . all the way.

Kerry Oh, no, no, no. I was in there for about maybe thirty, forty-five minutes, whatever, and I got cold feet because she was so aggressive, and I left.

And I didn't ever see or hear from her ever again until I'm arrested for her murder three months later, August of 1977.

Sound of a gavel. Lights up on Kerry's Defense, Kerry's Prosecutor, and Kerry's Judge. They speak facing the audience.

Kerry's Defense Since June 10, 1977, Tyler, Texas, has been screaming and crying for *someone* to answer to this crime –

Kerry's Prosecutor (*thick Texas accent*) The State of Texas would object to that being far beyond the scope of this case –

Kerry's Judge I am going to sustain that objection.

Courtroom freezes.

Kerry They had found a fingerprint of mine on her door frame.

Sandra And they had a fingerprint guy whose knowledge of fingerprints at that point was a six-month correspondence school –

Courtroom back in action.

Kerry's Prosecutor (*overlapping*) The lieutenant here is an expert fingerprint technologist. He will testify that he found a fingerprint belonging to the defendant, Kerry Max Cook. It is as clear, ladies and gentlemen, as the day when you put your footprint on your birth certificate. That officer didn't have any reason to lie. He will narrow the time element of the leaving of those fingerprints –

Kerry's Defense Objection, Your Honor.

Kerry (*to audience*) You *can't* date a fingerprint; it's scientifically impossible.

Kerry's Defense It cannot be proven what time those prints were made. This would place in the minds of the jurors that the defendant was there at the time of the murder!

Kerry's Judge Is that all you have?

Kerry's Defense Yes, ma'am.

Kerry's Judge Your motion is overruled.

Kerry That judge let them say, all through my trial, that I left that fingerprint there at the time of her murder

And this next part has all been hidden for twenty years: Linda, the victim, had been having an affair with Dr Whitfield, a professor of sciences over at the University, and *everyone* had just found out about it, he was fired from his job, lost his wife, lost his kids, whole big mess. And her roommate, Darla, had seen somebody in the apartment the night of the murder, who she said had silver hair, medium-short, touching-the-ears fashion, wearing white tennis shorts. Well, that's that Whitfield.

In her police report, Darla says she sees Whitfield in the apartment that night and says –

Lights up on Darla.

Darla Don't worry, it's only me.

Kerry – and goes to bed. But at the trial, she turns around and says –

Darla (*pointing*) That's the man right there.

Kerry – and points at me.

Lights down on Darla and courtroom.

Kerry And my lawyer didn't even argue with that. My court-appointed attorney was the former DA who jailed me twice before. He was paid five hundred dollars, and in Texas you get what you pay for.

Lights down on Kerry and Sandra, up on Delbert.

Delbert It's not easy to find some quiet place.
   Some grace. No time
   to talk about dreams
   in this world
   where ice
   is everywhere.

Lights down on Delbert, up on David.

David David Keaton.
   At the time they pulled me in, I was in high school.
I had a lotta thoughts of what I was gonna do, where
I was gonna go, where I should be, ten years from there,
you know. I was, as some might say, I was called to the
ministry.
   But I mean, the way they picked me up – me and some
friends was comin' from a movie that day and we saw a
big commotion, and we said, 'Man, what's goin' on?' So
we run down, and the cops are all round here, shinin'
their lights up on my grandmother's house.
   And we was just standin' there watchin', and the cop
says –

Lights up on Deputy.

Deputy Do any of y'all know David Keaton?

David And boy, here I am like a nut: 'I am he.'
   So they took me down to the station and interrogated
me, askin' me about this robbery, and I just kept sayin'
to them over and over, 'I don't know what you're talkin'
about. I don't know what you're talkin' about. I don't
know what you're talkin' about.' But they locked the
doors, they held me incommunicado, as you might say.
   When they first brought me into the jail, one of the
deputies asked the sheriff at that time –

29

Lights up on Sheriff Carroll.

Deputy (*southern accent*) You gonna keep him?

David And the sheriff said –

Sheriff Carroll (*thick southern accent*) You're goddamn right, we gonna keep him.

David The sheriff was running for re-election at the time, and this was a big unsolved crime, so he had to bring somebody in for it. And they're tellin' me what happened in the crime, who was standin' where and all of that, and I mean, I don't even know what the store looks like, and they're yellin' at me, tryin' to get me to describe it.

Lights dim slightly on David throughout the following.

Deputy This interview is being given with Deputy Sheriff H. M. Carroll. Mr Carroll, if you will, explain to me the events that took place at Luke's Grocery on September 18, 1970, as they relate to the case of David Keaton.

Sheriff Carroll Well, about two-thirty, Officer Khomas Revels and myself went in. I went over to the tobacco counter to get some chaw and he walked on back toward the milk case. And then I heard a nigger tell him, 'Get on over there, I ain't got no time to fool with you,' so I walked on around to where Khomas was at. And this boy, he had a gun, just said, 'Don't give us no trouble.' And he had, ah, kind of an Afro haircut, not a full Afro, but he looked like he was tryin' to grow him some Afro hair. And he had a little mustache, best I can remember – I mean everything was goin' so fast there. And the other one that was standin' over where they had about five or six customers tied down, he was around six foot tall. And the third son of a bitch – on his forehead, looked like he had, I don't know, you've seen them with kind of a scar sometimes?

30

Deputy Oh yeah.

Sheriff Carroll Anyway, they told us to give them our money. So we did, 'bout thirty-two dollars, and then they said, 'We want them watches, too.' Well, we didn't either one of us pull our watches off.

And they told us to lay down. So we did, and one of them, he reached over to get him some panty hose to tie us up with – but myself and Khomas, we came up and tackled them. Ain't nobody gonna be tyin' me up with no panty hose. And so the other one, he come runnin' down shootin' at us.

They must have shot eighteen or twenty bullets during the ruckus there, and the two hit me, and the two hit Khomas. And I could see that he was dead. (*Extended beat.*) And the niggers, they just disappeared.

Deputy Mr Carroll, in listening to these people talk in the store, did they have any type of accent? Did they sound like local people, or were they from out of state?

Sheriff Carroll Naw, they just sounded like regular niggers to me.

Lights down on Deputy and Sheriff Carroll, full up on David.

David And I was just eighteen, I didn't know the rules. And they kept on talkin', and they were threatenin' me, and all that. And I was afraid. I mean, they could go in there and beat you up, mess you up, hang you up, nobody'd ever hear nothin' else about you. And so I say, Okay, to prevent that, I'm gonna go ahead and confess to the crime. I know I'm tellin' the truth, and the witnesses are gonna know too, 'cause I just wasn't there and they would have seen that. So I'm like, I'm gonna let them go ahead, they gave me all the information already, so all I do is put some names to the spots and then we all can be free.

Lights down on David, up on Sunny.

Sunny Sunny Jacobs. (*Beat.*) In 1976, I was sentenced to death row, which for me wasn't a row at all, because I was the only woman in the country who had the sentence of death. So *I* suggested they put me in the same cell as my husband!

But let me start at the beginning. (*Beat.*)

When I was twenty-six, Jesse and I had been together for three years. We weren't officially married, but I considered him my husband, you know. Our daughter had just been born, and Jesse said he was gonna get himself a regular job, maybe painting murals or something, but he just needed to go to Florida one last time to do a little deal.

Now, I didn't want to know about this deal, because I knew it wasn't positive; it wasn't violent, but it wasn't positive. And finally he calls and says that the deal fell through, and not only is he broke and has no way home, but he's staying with some *girl*! So, of course, me, instead of saying, 'Well, when you get it together, me and the kids will be here waiting for you,' I said, 'I'll be right there to getcha!'

My son Eric was nine, and I was driving, shifting, singing, and nursing Tina all at the same time. It was like driving through the ten plagues, you know, the first being the oil leaking all over the road, and the final one – you know those lovebugs that smash themselves on your window?

So anyway, we get there, get Jesse, the car dies, and we're all stuck in Florida. And so Jesse says he'll ask this guy he knows if we can stay with him until we can scrape the money together to get home.

And that's when I met Walter Rhodes.

So we're all stuck in Florida, staying at Walter Rhodes's apartment. And it was a real sleazebag place; I mean, it sure seemed like he was doing illegal activities.

Lights up on Jesse and Rhodes.

Jesse Hey, Rhodes, we're gonna take off. Could you give us a lift to my friend's over in Broward County?

Rhodes I don't know, man, it's late. I don't know if I want to be on the road –

Jesse Come on, man, nothing ever happens in Broward.

Lights down on Jesse and Rhodes.

Sunny And it was so weird – my son Eric woke up screaming in the middle of the night. He had this nightmare that something terrible was going to happen to us. And it did.

Lights down on Sunny, up on Delbert.

Delbert
It's not easy
to feel good in winter winds
when ice is everywhere
and you just wanna sing . . . Copyright 1997,
    Delbert Tibbs . . .

I'm Delbert Tibbs.

I'm a child of the sixties and the seventies, right? So, much of the philosophy that people were motivated by during those times I was, and continue to be, motivated by. I have an on-going – an *abiding* interest in things philosophical and/or metaphysical; I won't say religious . . .

And so, you know, in 1972, I went to seminary for a year and a half, but the racism there was so pervasive you could cut it with a knife. So I decided that the seminary wasn't gonna take me where I wanted to go, so I dropped out and started roaming America. We called it 'tunin' in'. Tune in, turn on, an' drop out. And I haven't turned off for a long time.

So that's where I was at – and I happened to be in Florida when some crazy stuff happened, a guy was killed, a young woman was raped, and I happened to be in Florida.

And I knew that some folks were gonna say –

Lights up on Southern White Guy.

Southern White Guy Now what's this nigga doin' here, and who is he, an' why is he *here*?

Lights down on Southern White Guy.

Delbert – and so forth, but my attitude was fuck that, you know? I'm an American citizen, and I've served in the armed forces of the United States, and all that kinda shit.

The point I'm trying to make is that in my mind I decided that I was gonna be free in terms a my movements. That I was gonna go wherever I wanted to go, in these United States, an' whatever came out of that, if there was trouble, then I would deal with it when it came. And sure enough . . . (*Chuckles.*) sure enough, trouble came.

(*Beat.*) Because this *crime* had occurred, and I was on the highway in Florida, so I was stopped and questioned, and the captain wrote me out a note sayin' –

Lights up on White Cop 1.

White Cop 1 (*unnaturally fast robotic monotone*) This person was stopped by me on this date and I'm satisfied that he's not the person wanted in connection with the crimes that occurred in southern Florida.

Lights down on White Cop 1.

Delbert Now, initially, the girl who survived the thing described the murderer as a black man about five six, very dark complexion, with pockmarked skin and a bush Afro. (*Beat.*) Now that don't fit me no matter how you draw it – except racially. That's the only thing we had in common: we're both black men.

But now it's like two weeks or something after the crime has occurred, and they gotta find *somebody*, 'cause the small town is in hysterics, you know? There's a nigger running around killing white men and raping white women, and you can't have that. (*Beat.*) Understandably.

So anyway, the cops stopped me again, and I said, 'No, I'm not.' I said I was stopped in Florida –

Lights up on White Cop 1.

White Cop 1 (*again, unnaturally fast robotic monotone*) This person was stopped by me on this date and –

Lights down on White Cop 1, up on White Cop 2.

Delbert (*interrupting*) – and to the satisfaction of the Florida Highway Patrol, I'm not the person that you're looking for. He says, in effect –

White Cop 2 Bullshit.

Delbert He says –

White Cop 2 You're Delbert Tibbs, I have a warrant for your arrest.

Delbert And they arrested me in Mississippi.

Lights down on Delbert and White Cop 2, up on Robert and Georgia.

Robert (*to Georgia*) . . . I mean, I might as well be wearin' a sign that says ARREST ME. I'M BLACK.

Georgia (*to audience*) It's always somethin'. I mean it's not all police officers, it's not all white people, but it's those few that make the rest of them look so bad –

Robert (*to audience*) But I mean, hypothetically speaking, if me and a white woman have an altercation, the cop gonna say, 'Well, it's okay for her.' But for me, all she got to say is, 'He touched my breast. He touched my booty,' and there go the wildfire.

Georgia It's not only just whites; it's blacks too –

Robert (*interrupting*) Not to cut you off, but one night, me and a white guy, we were sitting at a gas station. We were just sitting there talking, and a white cop came back around to talk to us.

Lights up on White Cop 1 and Southern White Guy.

Robert And he didn't ask me was I having a problem, he asked the white guy was *he* having a problem. He says –

White Cop 1 I see both you guys talking and moving your hands.

Robert And you know, the black person talk with his hands, if you guys haven't noticed. The white guy, he said –

Southern White Guy No, me and Robert just sitting up here talking.

Robert And the cop said –

White Cop 1 Do you know Robert?

Southern White Guy Yeah, I been knowing him for the longest.

Robert But the cop said –

White Cop 1 Oh, I thought he was harassing you.

Georgia *Okay?!*

Lights down on White Cop 1 and Southern White Guy.

Robert I mean, God put everyone on earth – God put the ass, He put the fleas – but there's a lot of white people that make me upset. But I'm not gonna call them Crackers and go and get my cousin and all that.

Georgia (*sotto voce, overlapping*) No, don't get your cousin; your cousin *crazy*.

36

Robert I think if anyone have anything against anyone in this country, it should have been the Indians. But I do think now, these days, it's a lot better, especially in Mississippi, because if it wasn't, I'd be sittin' here sayin', 'Yes ma'am, Miss Daisy.' Maybe it's goin' away –

Georgia (*interrupting*) But Robert – (*to audience*) Okay, in my opinion, you never gonna get rid of it. My father taught me, things are passed down from generation to generation, and if the older generation teach the younger generation, then it ain't never gonna go away.

Lights down on Robert and Georgia, up on Delbert.

Delbert No time in this world to talk about dreams,
no space to place words in some lovely configuration;
deliberation is not the method
for passage through these woods
cold, tired
if you dream in this world
it is dangerous

Lights down on Delbert, up on Sunny.

Sunny My son Eric couldn't sleep because of the nightmare, and I just couldn't stay with Rhodes another night. So finally Rhodes agreed to give me, Jesse, and the kids a ride.

And we left, but the traffic got bad and it was getting late, so the decision was made to pull off the road until morning.

Dim light up on Black Cop, Jesse, Rhodes.

Sunny And according to the police reports, the cops came to do a routine check on the rest area. And when they look in the window, they see a gun between Rhodes's feet. They order him out of the car and ask for his ID. The policeman calls in the ID information, and then tells Rhodes –

Black Cop Stand over there, I'm finished with you.

Sunny And then they ask my husband Jesse to get out.

And then the police radio comes back with the announcement that Rhodes is on parole – and possession of a gun is a parole violation.

And that changed everything. The policeman drew his gun. He said –

Black Cop Okay, the next one to move is dead.

Sunny It all happened so fast, you know. I just ducked down to cover the kids.

Sound of four loud gunshots.

Sunny And then it was silence. I mean *dead silence*. There wasn't an earthly sound.

And then Rhodes runs around the front of the police car with a gun in his hand, and he's saying –

Rhodes Come on, we're gonna take the police car!

Sunny I mean, Rhodes had just killed two policemen, had a gun, and was telling us to get in the police car. And, you know, people say, 'Why didn't you just refuse to go?' And I think, You've never been at the other end of a gun, have you?

So we get in the police car. We couldn't speak.

Sound of cars honking / helicopters.

We were kidnapped at that point, and we just didn't dare.

But then all of a sudden, the traffic gets terrible, and you can hear the helicopters, and I know there must be a roadblock. 'Hey, we're gonna be *rescued*! Help is on the way, you know, the cavalry!'

And out of nowhere, Rhodes make a sharp left to try and avoid the roadblock –

Sound of heavy gunfire.

– and this whole line of policemen opens fire on the car. The car was literally bouncing with all the bullets. So again I cover the kids. And finally we crash.

Sound of crash / sirens.

And a bunch of cops surround us, and I'm trying to explain that we were kidnapped, but they just wouldn't listen.

Lights shift; we are now in Sunny's interrogation room.

White Cop 1 All right. Sonia, or do you want me to call you Sunny?

Sunny It doesn't matter.

White Cop 2 (*interrupting, to Sunny*) Do you know what the date today is?

Sunny I think it's the twentieth.

White Cop 2 Is it Friday?

White Cop 1 (*jumping in*) Let me inject one thing here. Are you aware of the fact that you have been charged and arrested on first-degree murder?

Sunny (*beat*) You just told me now.

Lights down on Sunny and Cops, up on Gary.

Gary I took a polygraph test around midnight. They wouldn't let me sleep, wouldn't let me lie down – and the polygraph examiner said he cannot pass me because of flat lines due to *fatigue*. Well, *duh*, it's midnight, I'd been under questioning now for six hours, and my parents had just been *murdered*.

About one a.m., they got three or four photos of my parents with their heads pulled back – you could look down their throats – and the detective's yelling –

Lights up on Cops.

White Cop 1 How could you do this?

White Cop 2 (*overlapping*) How could you kill this woman?

White Cop 1 (*overlapping*) The person who gave birth to you!

Lights down on Cops.

Gary And this is how the interrogation went. I was in such a vulnerable and suggestible state from finding my parents and not knowing what happened. I was emotionally distraught, I was physically exhausted. I was confused. I had fifteen cups of coffee. I was spaced-out. And the police used that. They said they had all the evidence, that they didn't even *need* my confession. They said they had bloody fingerprints, the weapon, everything.

I was brainwashed, man. They told me –

Lights up on White Cop 1 and White Cop 2.

White Cop 1 *and* **White Cop 2** (*in unison, very friendly*) We can't lie to you, or we'd lose our jobs.

Gary They seemed very sincere, too. Very believable. They started making me think I had a blackout and actually done it. I said, Look, if I killed my parents, I want to know about it.

So I said, Okay, if I could construct the situation in my mind – (*Small beat.*) I finally volunteered to give what they call a 'vision statement' – a hypothetical account of what I would have done if I had killed my parents –

Cops To try and jog your memory.

Gary – to try and jog my memory.

Lights down on White Cop 1 and White Cop 2. Gary begins 'vision statement,' trying to put it all together.

Well, I guess I would've gotten up that morning –

Lights up on White Cop 1, testifying on the stand. Sure of what he's saying. His lines overlap tightly with Gary's – in the following section, the actors should speak over the ends of each other's lines.

White Cop 1 The defendant stated that he got up that morning –

Gary And my mom would've been out in the trailer –

White Cop 1 – and that he looked outside and saw his mother in the trailer.

Gary Then I woulda gotten dressed – and I would've had to have a knife in my pocket or something –

White Cop 1 And he indicated he put his pants on, and he had a knife in his pants pocket.

Gary I guess I would've gone over to the trailer she was in –

White Cop 1 Then he walked up to the trailer and stepped onto the porch.

Gary – and walked in –

White Cop 1 He said he opened the door, he walked in.

Gary I would've had to have reached out toward my mom –

White Cop 1 He reached up and he grabbed his mother with his left hand and cut her throat with his right.

Lights down on White Cop 1.

Gary (*beat*) I never would've hurt her.

Lights shift.

They used that vision statement for a *confession*.
    And they wouldn't let me say anything besides how I would've done it. Anytime I tried to say anything else,

they would just holler at me, and holler at me, and holler at me.

After I made the statement about my mom, I cried for about three minutes, and then I told them how I would have killed my father. And then I said – I *told* them – 'This is just hypothetical. I have absolutely no memory of any of this.'

The autopsies showed that everything I said in those statements was wrong. But nothing was written down, nothing was recorded. At the trial, they said that I was never under arrest, I was free to go at any time, that I had voluntarily 'chatted' with them for *twelve hours*, and then suddenly blurted out facts that only the killer would know.

Lights down on Gary, up on Delbert.

Delbert Well, yeah, man, it definitely has an effect on you for people to lock you up. First of all, it shows you they have the power to do it, and then they tell you they're gonna kill you, you know, and you're inclined to believe them. (*Chuckles.*) So it definitely messes with your sense of personal power, you know what I'm saying?

Lights up on Sunny, down on Delbert.

Sunny (*to audience*) So I actually did at first try to lie, and I told the cops I didn't know these people, I was just a hitchhiker. Stupid. Because of course they think you're lying because you did something. But I was just scared.

Lights shift; we are back in Sunny's interrogation room. Cops keep the pressure intensely, relentlessly high on Sunny throughout the following.

White Cop 2 Let me ask you point blankly. Who shot the Highway Patrolman and the other officer?

Sunny I don't know.

White Cop 1 Did you shoot the Highway Patrolman?

42

Sunny No!

White Cop 2 Sunny, did you shoot anyone?

Sunny No.

White Cop 1 (*yelling*) *DO YOU KNOW IF SOMEONE WAS SHOT?!*

Sunny I'm *sorry*. People were shot. The patrolmen were shot and that's what this is all about – I don't know –

White Cop 2 (*jumping down Sunny's throat*) Well, how do you know that the two policemen are dead?

Sunny You said. That's what we're here for.

White Cop 2 Okay. We advised you that they were dead because we had – (*He continues to talk over Sunny's next line.*)

Sunny I didn't see. I didn't see –

White Cop 2 (*talking over her*) – we had to read you your rights and it's imperative that you relate the facts of this to the best of your ability. Something caused you to be very disturbed. What was that something?

Sunny (*breaking down*) This is very upsetting because how does – this guy, he told – he just told us to sit in the car, you know – and I'll stay here and I won't make any calls and I – I haven't done anything except the wrong choice of people and I –

White Cop 1 (*very close to Sunny*) But you do want to co-operate with the state of Florida?

Sunny Yeah, I –

White Cop 2 You're not *being* too co-operative, because you're saying a lot of things you don't even remember and yet you were there. You were there, Sunny.

Sunny I'm sorry, I – I know, but I never had anything like this happen to me before. I just – I don't want to be blamed for something that I had nothing to do with and I don't want them to take the kids away and I – 'cause the baby's crying and crying and crying and Eric's scared and I – I do want to help. I –

White Cop 1 All right, Sunny, I want you to help us.

Sunny Because I don't – I don't know what this guy was up to and I don't want to be pulled into it, but do you understand I'm trying to co-operate with –

White Cop 1 (*condescending to her*) Yes, sweetheart, I fully understand this.

Sunny And if I can't tell you everything you need to know please don't be angry with me.

White Cop 2 Okay, okay. (*Beat.*) Is there anything you care to add to your statement at this time?

Sunny I can't think of anything but if I do I will.

White Cop 1 (*an accusation*) All right, are the answers you've given true and accurate to the best of your knowledge?

Beat as Sunny considers whether to tell the truth, then yelling.

ANSWER ME!

Sunny (*lying*) Yes.

Lights down on Cops; we are out of Sunny's interrogation room.

And what I didn't know was at the same moment I was being questioned and Jesse was being questioned, was that Rhodes, from his hospital bed, was negotiating a deal. He'd been in prison before, he knew how the system

44

worked. And so he was claiming that he didn't do it –
we did.

*Lights down on Sunny; up on State Attorney and
Rhodes.*

State Attorney Okay, Mr Rhodes. Who had the gun in
their hands when the first shot was fired?

Rhodes (*extremely helpful*) When the gun first went off,
Sonia was the one holding the gun. (*then explaining*) This
is to the best of my knowledge, I am not one hundred per
cent sure. To the best of my knowledge, she fired two
shots, I believe then Jesse pulled the gun from her and
shot him one more time and then he shot the other cop
twice.

State Attorney Let me recap this now. To the best of your
recollection, Sonia fired?

Rhodes First.

State Attorney It is your testimony here that Sonia fired
the first three shots at the Florida Highway Patrolman?

Rhodes Either the first two or three.

State Attorney Two, or three?

Rhodes Two for sure.

State Attorney And then what took place?

Rhodes Then I started to go toward my car, to get in,
it didn't even enter into my mind, but Jesse said, 'Get in
the police car. We have got to get out of here,' or something,
and I said, 'No,' you know, '*what happened*?!' Anyway I
did get in the police car, I was damn near in shock myself.

State Attorney Thank you.

Rhodes No problem.

Lights down on Rhodes and State Attorney, up on Delbert.

Delbert So I'm sitting there in Mississippi. After a couple days of being locked up, I decided I would waive extradition. Now this was because of my spiritual growth. A friend of mine has something he calls his 'nigger radar', right, which sort of alerts him when, as he quotes Darth Vader, when there's a 'disturbance in the force'.

But I'm operating on another thing, you know, 'cause a lotta the *tension* I had felt regarding race had sorta been washed away. I had achieved some sort of spiritual . . . plateau, if you will, by living out on the road.

I wasn't expecting any problems. I had been befriended by all kinda people – mostly white folks, 'cause there weren't no black folks around. I hitchhiked across Texas, which is as big as Russia, you know what I'm sayin'? And I got *one* ride from a brother. Brother picked me up. He said –

Lights up on Black Guy 1.

Black Guy 1 Man, you know brothers don't hitchhike out here too much.

Delbert I know, but I don't have any money, what am I gonna do.

Lights down on Black Guy 1.

Delbert Anyway, I waived extradition to Florida, meaning I voluntarily went back. If I hadn't done that, I don't think I would've ever gone to death row, 'cause the state of Florida really didn't have a case. Nobody had seen me there, there was no connection between me and the place where the crime occurred, fingerprints, none a that – 'cause I *wasn't there*.

And in Florida, as in most places, the jury is chosen from the voting records. And this is 1974 – black people had only had the right to vote since 1965 – and this is a backwater town, where it's run sorta like a plantation and the folks in charge are the folks in charge, right?

And as I sometimes tell people, if you're accused of a sex crime in the South and you're black, you probably shoulda done it, you know, 'cause your ass is gonna be guilty. And they found me guilty.

Lights down on Delbert, up on courtroom; sound of a gavel being hit.

Robert's Judge (*thick southern accent, bangs gavel*) Gentlemen, you have the right to remain silent. Anything you say can and will be used against you in a court of law. If you cannot afford an attorney, one will be appointed for you. Does everyone understand that? (*Beat.*) You can answer that question. (*Small beat.*) Yes?

Murmurs from seated group.

Good. Robert Hayes.

Court Attorney He's in the first chair, Your Honor.

Robert's Judge Mr Hayes.

No response, then beat.

Mr Hayes.

Robert (*very softly, head down*) Yeah.

Court Attorney Your Honor, he hears the court. He just doesn't want to show his face to the cameras, which is –

Robert's Judge I want him to respond to me. Mr –

Robert (*looking up*) I *said* yes.

Robert's Judge Okay. Mr Hayes, you're charged with murder in the first degree. We find probable cause the accused committed the offense. He'll be held on no bond.

47

Court Attorney Your Honor, Mr Hayes has indicated that he does not wish to speak to anyone from law enforcement without an attorney present.

Robert's Judge Okay, Mr Hayes, can you afford a lawyer?

Robert No.

Robert's Judge Are you employed?

Robert I *was*.

Robert's Judge Do you own any property?

Robert No.

Robert's Judge Do you have any bank accounts?

Robert No.

Robert's Judge Do you have an automobile?

Robert No.

Robert's Judge The court will find that Mr Hayes is indigent. Appoint the public defender to represent him.

Sound of a gavel.

Court Attorney Thank you.

Lights down on courtroom, up on Delbert.

Delbert This is a weird country, man, it really is. It always amazes me when I talk about this. I say, 'How do you figure this, now: all these guys, they been to Vanderbilt and to Yale and to Princeton and Harvard and shit, they look at the same information and they come up with diametrically opposite conclusions. Figure that out.'

So it doesn't have anything to do with one's intelligence; it has to do with one's preconceptions, with one's *tendencies*, and how one looks at other human *beings* – you see, *that's* what it's about.

*Lights down on Delbert; up on Kerry, Kerry's
Prosecutor, Kerry's Defense, and Kerry's Judge.*

Kerry So they had a lead that the victim's boyfriend,
Professor Whitfield, might have done the murder. But
they didn't go after him; they went after me. They said
the crime was done by a homosexual maniacal murderer
who hated women. The prosecution accused me of bein'
a homosexual – before the jury –

Kerry's Prosecutor (*thick Texas accent*) A young woman
lies in her grave not far from this courtroom, butchered,
because of Kerry Max Cook's warped homosexual lust
for blood and perversion –

Kerry's Defense Objection, Your Honor. The defendant's
alleged homosexuality has nothing to do with the
allegations in the murder indictment.

Kerry's Judge Objection will be overruled.

Kerry's Defense We would then request an instruction to
the jury that they cannot consider –

Kerry's Judge That motion is also overruled –

Kerry's Defense We would then request the Court to
declare a mistrial in this case –

Kerry's Judge *Overruled.* Proceed, Counsel.

*Lights slowly go out on Kerry's Defense and Judge
during the Prosecutor's speech. Lights remain up on
Kerry and Prosecutor.*

Kerry's Prosecutor Thank you, Your Honor.
(*to audience; with crescendoing fervor*) Ladies and
gentlemen of the jury. I would be remiss in my duty if
I did not show you every last grotesque detail, because
the killer sits right before you in this courtroom and it is
time for twelve good people from this county to put that

man on the scrap heap of humanity where he belongs. He has a warped perversion and he will not reason with you. The victim was a young woman just beginning to realize her dreams, and he butchered her body. This is the kind of sick perversion that turns Kerry Max Cook on.

You people have no right to even submit prison guards to the kind of risk that man poses. Think about it. Do you want to give this pervert his butcher knife back? Now, we must look upon it as putting a sick animal to sleep. Kerry Max Cook has forfeited his right to walk among us. He no longer has rights.

So let's let all the freaks and perverts and murderous homosexuals of the world know what we do with them in a court of justice. That we take their lives.

Lights out on Kerry and Kerry's Prosecutor; up on Sunny.

Sunny My husband Jesse was tried first, and he had a past record, from when he was seventeen years old, and his trial lasted four days. We both had, of course, no good attorneys, no dream team, no expert witnesses, and so he was convicted, and sentenced to death.

My trial came later. I thought, Surely that won't happen to *me*. I mean, I was a hippie. I'm one of those peace-and-love people. I'm a *vegetarian*! How could you possibly think I would kill someone?

And so I thought I'd go in, they'd figure out I didn't kill anyone, and they'd let it go. But that's not how it works. There was prosecutorial misconduct, there was hiding of evidence that would have proven I didn't do it. The jury wasn't even allowed to know that Rhodes accepted a plea bargain of three life sentences in exchange for his testimony! Now, I don't think three life sentences is a bargain. Nobody *I* know would think it's a bargain . . .

And I didn't have any investigators, I didn't have any expert witnesses, I didn't have thousands of dollars. My parents said, 'Well, you know, we were told we could try and get you a better lawyer, but you *have* a lawyer – they've *appointed* you one – so it's okay.' We didn't know.

Lights down on Sunny, up on David, David's Prosecutor, and David's Defense.

David's Prosecutor The State respectfully submits to this jury that in that grocery store David Keaton actually fired at Sheriff Carroll in order to come to the assistance of his co-defendant, who was in the process of cold-bloodedly murdering and killing Officer Khomas Revels. It's just as clear and simple as that. As a matter of fact, that is actually the truth.

David's Defense It was a quiet and peaceful Sunday night before David Keaton, then eighteen years old, was speedily whisked away to Quincy Jail. He was not told the reason for his arrest, nor was his family informed.

David's Prosecutor They're gonna tell you that all of Keaton's answers were suggested by the officers, that he was framed. Not by one officer, now; not by two officers, but by three or more state and county law-enforcement officers.

David's Defense He was questioned without benefit of counsel, despite his request to his interrogators to call his mother and obtain legal assistance. At eleven p.m., Keaton was taken to the jail in Tallahassee, where questioning resumed and continued until the next morning.

David's Prosecutor Now, Keaton could have said in his statement anything he wanted to. There was nobody making those defendants say anything, and this jury knows anyway that of course that would be impossible, impractical. You just can't *make* somebody say something; nobody can!

David's Defense There is a law in this state that any person arrested shall be taken without delay and have the charges read in open court. The defendant was arrested on a Sunday. Well, this courthouse is open on Monday, and it's open on Tuesday, Wednesday, Thursday, too. The defendant was not taken before a judge until Friday, although he had been arrested the Sunday before.

Now, I have nothing but respect for the deputy sheriffs, but I recognize, too, that it was a member of their staff that was killed. Wouldn't it be understandable for them to be more . . . *emotionally involved* in the investigation?

Lights down on David, David's Prosecutor, and David's Defense, up on Sunny.

Sunny They tell you exactly how they're gonna do it. They're gonna send twenty-two hundred volts of electricity through your body until you're dead. And then they ask you if you have anything to say to that, and really it's kind of dumbfounding. So after the judge read the sentence, I just said, 'Are you finished?' I didn't have anything to say. What do you say? How can you say anything to that?

Sound of a cell door slamming shut. Lights up on Delbert, down on Sunny.

Delbert I don't remember any of my dreams from when I was on death row. I almost never recall my dreams, which I am absolutely fascinated by.

When I was at the University of Chicago, I took part in a laboratory experiment. They were running a test to see if creative people's dreams differ from those who are less creative. And so of course, it appealed to the ego in me, thinking somebody thought I was creative.

So you go to bed in the lab and they are monitoring your respiration and your REM and so forth. And they would wake me up over the microphone, and it always sounded to me like one of the Nazi doctors 'cause he had an accent, you know, he would be like, 'MISTA TIBBS, YOU VERE DREAMINK.' And I wanted to say, No shit.

But the fascinating thing was, when the motherfuckers hooked me up, they put the receptors by your ears, right exactly at the same place they do when they're getting ready to execute your ass.

Lights down on Delbert, up on Sunny.

Sunny Instead of sending me to be Jesse's cellmate, they decided to clear out an entire disciplinary unit at the women's prison. It's a very old prison, it's like a dungeon-type place. It was six steps from the door to the toilet bowl – you could stretch out your arms and touch both walls. They take your clothes; they give you a number, so basically they're taking . . . who you *are* from you. You no longer have a name, you're a number. You're locked inside this *tomb*. It's like you're thrown to the bottom of the well.

Lights down on Sunny, up on David.

David There was one woman, lived across the street when I was a little boy, she had a goiter on her neck. And I was sayin', 'Lord, if I only had the power of the Spirit, I would go lay my hands on her and her illness would disappear.' And that's all I want, just to let the Spirit be operatin' through me, whether it be knowledge, discernment, speak the Word, or whatever. (*to God*) I would love to just do that before I die.

I had a relationship to God when I got in here, but somehow I've lost it. I guess I'm still reachin' out to find it – you know, I said some nights now I wanna light me a couple candles, lay back and just meditate, 'cause they say the kingdom of God is within you, isn't it? You know, everybody lookin' for something outward, but then, that light's *within* you, that voice we speak to . . . (*whispering God's voice*) 'C'mon, boy.'

Give you the chills when I say that, right?

Lights down on David, up on Kerry.

Kerry You know, when I was in there, I saw a hundred and forty-one guys go down. All's I got to do is pick up the newspaper, turn on the news, 'Such and such becomes the two hundred and twenty-second inmate executed resulting from capital punishment,' and I hear the name and I say, 'Oh my God,' 'cause I know him. I mean, I don't just *know* him, I *ate* with him, I *cried* with him, we used to play basketball and talk about 'Man, you're gonna go free.'

You know, I got a book, a book about Texas death row, and seriously, this book is what, five years old, and everyone in here has been executed. I can go through that book, one by one, and point out every face in here that's gone.

Inmate Executed.

Sound of a switch being thrown.

Inmate Executed.

Sound of a switch being thrown.

Inmate Executed.

Sound of a switch being thrown.

Kerry And you know, at a capital trial, the prosecutors always say, 'He's dangerous, he's a maniac, the sick, twisted murderer.' But I'm no different from you – I mean, I wasn't a street thug, I wasn't trash, I came from a good family – if it happened to me, man, it can happen to anyone.

Lights down on Kerry, up on Gary.

Gary I was in X house – the execution house. That place was like somethin' out of a movie. There were no guards.

They would just open your cell door and let you run around. I guess they figured you were gonna die anyway, so why not.

So you can walk around through this dimly lit series of corridors, and through the observation room, into the execution room. That's where the phone was that all of us used. Which was also the phone that the governor would use to call in and stop an execution.

The whole place was run by gangs, you know, there was ongoing warfare between the different factions. And the only gang open to white guys was the Northsiders – which is basically made up of the Aryan Nation and the Skinheads. So I had no gang protection. So I kept to myself a lot. Killed a lot of time on my own.

One way I killed time, was I found a sewing needle stuck in a concrete wall. Somebody had smuggled it in. So I taught myself embroidery.

You'd take extra clothing – the blue jeans made real good blue thread. And I was lucky – I had kept my old yellow jumpsuit that they gave me to wear when I first went in. So that gave me yellow. You take your sheet apart, that gives you white. So I had three colors of thread, just from unraveling cloth. I made myself a tote bag I'd take to chow hall, and I embroidered flowers on it. I put bell-bottoms on a couple of my prison blues, made a Calvin and Hobbes patch I put on my hat. They confiscated that one.

Lights down on Gary, up on Robert.

Robert The electric chair was downstairs and I was upstairs, and every Wednesday morning they cranked that electric chair up and you could hear it buzz.

And when they served breakfast, you gotta have sharp ears to hear that front door open, 'cause if you oversleep, the roaches and the rats come and eat your breakfast, and that's the God's honest truth.

And the guards – I think nine times out of ten, the average person that became a guard, the only way I can see it, when he grew up he was a little runt and then the bigger guy would mess with him and all of that. And then they grow up and they wanna do that too.

When I was in there, one day, this officer was harassing my neighbor and I was a witness. And the other inmate, he wanted to write the officer up, he asked me –

Lights up on Black Inmate.

Black Inmate Hey, Robert, would you sign this statement?

Robert I said, I told him, yeah.

But a couple of days later, the officer came back to work, and something just told me to pay attention to him.

Lights up on White Guard.

Robert And sure enough, this officer, he read that statement, he gonna get back at me. He gonna spit off in my tea. And I *seen* him spit off in my tea. And so I said, (*looking at Guard*) 'Now why would you do that?'

White Guard Do what? I didn't do that.

Robert Hold on, I'm gonna prove it to you.

(*to audience*) And I went and got me a piece of toilet paper, (*miming*) twisted it up, and put it directly on top of that tea. And I went round it. And I said, (*to Guard*) 'Now what is that? You can have my tea. You can take that shit back, MOTHERFUCKER.'

Lights down on Guard. Lights shift on Robert.

Robert (*with increasing intensity*) Robert E. Hayes, number nine five one nine eight one seven, May 21, 1996.

Judge Kaplan,

I am writing to you in regards to some matters which I am having in this jail. The superintendent decline to answer any of my grievances, so I am makin' you aware of this before I get charged this time for something I DID do. The problem is this Officer Santiago, who has constantly been provoking me. He come into my cell and toss my legal papers around, just tryin' to provoke me to fight him.

And today, he got classification to relocate me to the dayroom of a special wing for drug offenders. And by law, they isn't supposed to have anyone sleeping in the dayroom, no matter what wing it's in.

With my luck, some other inmate, some snitch, will get one of my legal briefs while I am sleeping, call the state, say, 'Robert Hayes confessed to me,' so he can get himself a deal, and say, 'If you let me out, I'll testify against him.' And you, Judge Kaplan, will believe that fuck shit.

So Judge, I am askin' you to grant me an order stating that me and the stated officer be kept away from one another, because I am *not* goin' to take *any more* of his *bullshit*!

(*Small beat.*) But thank you for your time. I'm sure I'll see you on another charge if you refuse to keep Santiago away from me.

Robert Hayes.

Lights up on Georgia.

Georgia And, okay, some snitch *did* get ahold of one of his legal briefs. Just like Robert said.

Lights down on Robert and Georgia, up on Kerry.

Kerry So, uh, they accused me of bein' a homosexual, and that got into the media that got to death row even before I got there, so in prison, uh, uh – I was uh, uh . . . I had three guys pull a train on me . . . and they raped me, and sodomized me, and they carved 'good p-u-s-s-y' on my behind. And it's there all over my body, it's cut so deep I can't – plastic surgery won't remove it, it's not a

57

tattoo, and I attempted suicide a couple times with this whole little war I was fighting: on the one side, the criminal justice system, and then on the western front, I'm fighting with fear of my life with these inmates every day.

Lights up on Delbert.

Delbert Needless to say, Job is one of my favorite biblical figures.

Lights down on Kerry.

I don't know if I have the patience of Job – but I hope I have his faith. Even if you got a teeny-weeny bit, it's big. The shit is hard to come by, you know what I'm sayin'?

But faith or not, I realized a long time ago, if I internalized all the anger, and all the pain, and all the hurt, I'd be dead already – they wouldn't even have to execute me.

Lights down on Delbert, up on David.

David When I was inside, one time, I felt this feelin' came over me where I felt the longin' of God for His people, I felt His love for His people, His desire for His people not to be cast aside. You know, I felt all this, and here I was on death row. It was so heavy. God, it was a burden on me.

And I was feelin' all this, and we went outside for recreation, and in the yard out there, you have a little basketball court, shuffleboard court, and there's a curtain up with the electric chair showin'. You look right up there, you can see the chair. You know, even if you playin', they gotta remind you that you still gonna die, 'cause here's the chair.

Sound of thunderclap and rain.

David But then it starts stormin', man.

I looked up, raise my hand, and I said, 'In the name of Jesus, I command this rain to stop.'

Sound of rain swooshing, then stopping.

This guy says, 'Man, you do it one more time, I'm gonna become a believer!' So it started again –

Sound of thunder and rain.

So I said it again. 'In the name of Jesus, I command this rain to stop.'

Sound of rain swooshing, then stopping.

It stopped. He said, 'Man, you do it *one more time* –'
So it started back . . . same thing.

Sound of thunder and rain.

'In the name of Jesus, I command this rain to stop.'

Sound of rain swooshing, then stopping.

But this time, he didn't say nothin'. He just looked at me like 'Hmm,' you know.

But it didn't rain any more, until we finished playin', and we had to go back inside. And when the last man stepped through the door, the whole world just burst open.

Sound of thunder and rain.

It rained for the rest of the night.

Lights down on David, up on Sunny. Rain fades slowly over the beginning of Sunny's speech.

Sunny I have fifteen years' worth of letters between me and Jesse. I saved not only the letters but the envelopes, because anything that he touched, or that he wrote on, or that he licked with his tongue, I was keeping. I didn't even read his letters when I first got them; I would carry 'em around with me for a while. Just to hold it. I'd see if he put the stamp on right side up or upside down. That was part of his message, too.

And then I'd open it and I wouldn't read it for content; I would just look at it to see: did he look like he was happy when he wrote it, or sad? Did the writing slant upward or downward? Oh, it's big round open letters, he must have been having a good day. Oh, it's very tight writing; I can see he must have been having some problems. I would just savor the whole thing, and *then* I'd read it.

We carried on a fairly full life in our letters, actually, including our sex life. Oh yeah.

Laughter.

You know, you have to send your letters out unsealed so that they can read them to see that there's no escape plans or whatever. So we got ourselves little Japanese dictionaries, and we used the Japanese language for our lovemaking, because we wanted to have some privacy.

Lights up on Jesse.

Jesse Sept. 30, 1976.

My Dearest Sunny,

I love you. It's about eleven p.m. now. I'm sitting here on my bunk. The TV is on with the sound off and on the channel that is just fuzzy so that I can use it for light. I'm reading *King Lear* and *Hamlet*, if you can believe that. I've been studying too much law lately and need to give my head something relaxing, too. I received your beautiful letter and . . . two pictures of the kids. We're so lucky. I love you so much. You're my woman, as close as my breath. You're the strongest female I've ever known. Hand and glove, you know?

Never be lonesome; we're only separated by miles. This won't last, either, believe that. I sure would like to speak to you alone, let's say for a few hours.

Hito banju kimiulo ikasetai
Kimito hitotsuni naritai

My place or yours. And don't worry, I'm on the case, lover.
I love you, Mama.
Jesse.

Lights down on Jesse.

Sunny And so we had this life, you know; this little
world together. I existed on those letters.

Lights down on Sunny, up on Kerry.

Kerry I was holding on for my brother. I can't tell you how
close we were, he wasn't just a big brother, I *worshiped*
him; he was my *role model*, he was everything I wasn't –
he didn't smoke pot, he made straight As in school – and
I was the black sheep of the family. My brother was
always trying to rescue me, very strict on me –

Lights up on Doyle.

Doyle No, Kerry, I'm gonna *lose* you, I'm gonna *lose*
you, you're gonna get hurt.

Kerry – and then there I was, sitting on death row.
   He was taking up for me my whole life. I was just
always a real soft sensitive person, you know, and I guess
I had so many girlfriends 'cause I was so sensitive, I don't
mean girlfriends like girls *sexually*; I mean friends that
are girls.
   And so my brother – the last time I touched him was
at the Smith County jail – he reached in and held my
hand and was crying and said –

Doyle It's not over, Kerry, 'cause you're not gonna die,
you're gonna get out.

Kerry I was the baby of the family and my brother
would come visit me and I would have these black eyes
and stuff, you know, and he said –

Doyle I want you to tell me who did this to you, I'm going to talk to the warden.

Kerry (*to Doyle*) You don't understand, you'll get me killed, that's called snitching; that's the worst thing you can do.

(*to audience*) So I forced my brother – when he thought he could help me, I took that away from him, too, saying, 'You can't help me; I'm on my own now.' And so, uh . . . he started drinking.

The guy had it all, man, he was a senior supervisor at this huge corporation company, and he fell into a bottle, lost his wife, lost his kids. He'd sit around in a dark room and get drunk and talk about his little brother, why isn't he coming home. He put himself right on death row with me.

And he's workin' as an assistant manager at a McDonald's in downtown Jacksonville, and there's this guy named Jeff works there. Jeff said that my brother liked him because my brother told him –

Lights up on Jeff.

Jeff *and* **Kerry** You're a lot like my little brother Kerry.

Kerry And that's how they got to be friends.

So anyway, one night after work they go to this club in Tyler, Texas, and they're shooting pool. You know how you get when you're drinking beer and you're hot with the stick.

And right now, it's closing and my brother's running the table on this one last guy – and he says to Jeff –

Doyle You go, I'll be out there in a minute.

Kerry And Jeff's walking out of the club, and there were these two black guys sitting on the table, and one of them's wearing sunglasses, and Jeff reaches up – he's just playing – takes the glasses, and puts them on –

Jeff mimics Stevie Wonder.

Kerry – and mimics Stevie Wonder. And the guy says –

Lights up on Black Guy 2.

Black Guy 2 Say, what's up on you, man?

Kerry And this guy jumps off the table and gets real aggressive, and he's like –

Black Guy 2 I'm gonna bring a world of hurt to him.

Kerry And so about this time, my brother walks up and says –

Doyle Hey, hey, man –

Kerry My brother's really laid-back, you know. He wasn't a violent dude – I mean, he was a real laid-back, compassionate person. But Jeff just says –

Jeff Man, fuck these people.

Kerry And walks out. So my brother follows him outside.

Beat. Lights shift.

Kerry It's December 27, 1997. It's really cold that night, and my brother and Jeff are both trying to get in the car but the locks are frozen, and this pickup truck pulls up behind my brother, and Jeff says –

Jeff Hey – watch out!

Kerry My brother turns around, and this guy, he got out of the truck with his hand behind his back and he says –

Black Guy 2 Whatcha gonna do for me, white boy, you gonna call me nigger? Whatcha gonna do for me?

Kerry There was all kinds of people standing around, and my brother told him –

Doyle Hey, look, man, we've all been drinking tonight – this is nothin' to have no misunderstanding about.

Tomorrow morning you're gonna wake up and laugh about this.

Kerry And he says –

Black Guy 2 Fuck you, man.

Kerry And he brings from around his back a big ol' forty-four Magnum and he shoots him.

Sound of a loud, long gunshot.

Kerry And uh, uh, my brother – so weird, man – he rose up and stood up, and Jeff walked over to him and he couldn't even tell he was shot, his eyes were fixated looking straight ahead. And Jeff said –

Jeff Man, you okay? Man, you okay?

Kerry And blood started pouring out of my brother's nose and he fell . . . and he died on that parking lot.

Lights down on Doyle and Jeff.

Kerry And uh . . . with me being on death row, the DA was reluctant to take it to trial – she said the defense would claim that my brother had bragged that he had a brother on death row and he was bad.

And so they got my mom and dad to agree to a plea bargain, and the guy who killed my brother got ten years. And he got out in three.

My mother would look me in the eye and tell me that I'm responsible for my brother's murder. That if it weren't for me going to death row, he'd still be here. She would tell me that. I know it's going to sound corny there, but – and I mean it – every day that goes by I wished I could tell him how much I love him. So while you've got it, man, never take it for granted, 'cause you never know.

Lights down on Kerry, up on Sunny.

Sunny First I had to decide, This is bullshit. I am not going to let them do this to me. 'Cause if you sit there, rubbing two sticks together and crying on your sticks, they're never gonna make a spark. But, you know, if you stop feeling sorry for yourself, just because you're determined not to believe in hopelessness, then a spark happens, and then you just keep fanning that little spark until you got a flame.

And I realized that it was like a big trick. That I wasn't just a little lump of flesh that they could put in a cage. And I decided that I would have faith, that there was some power out there greater than them, to which I could make my appeal.

Now, you people that don't believe, you could say I was like Dumbo and I put this feather in my nose and I flew because I could fly anyway.

Or you could say that there really is something out there, and if we have faith in it and we appeal to it, it will answer us. And maybe we're both right. I don't know.

Lights down on Sunny, up on Robert.

Robert Well, see, before I went to prison, I had a dream about prison – and I seen death row, I seen the inside, and I seen myself get out. And 'cause a that dream, I always said, I'm gonna get a new trial. And sure enough, one day, I get awakened by all this commotion. All the inmates, they get up in the vents, hollerin' –

Lights up on Inmates.

All Men (*ad lib*) Man, you got a new trial! Damn, Robert, you gonna go free! You on the radio! Turn on the radio! (*Etc.*)

Cellmate Put the radio on!

Robert Well, I put the radio on.

And later that day, my lawyer came, and she said to me –

Lights down on Inmates, up on Female Lawyer.

Female Lawyer Now, you know, Robert, if you lose, you can go back to death row.

Robert And I said, (*to Lawyer*) 'Well, now, accordin' to that dream, I'm gonna go free.'
    And she said –

Female Lawyer (*to Robert*) You gonna put all your trust in a dream?

Robert And I said, 'Yep.' (*Small beat.*)

Lights up on Prosecutor, Georgia, and Ex-Boyfriend.

Robert My lawyer had found a record that said that in the girl's hand when she died was some white-people hair, red hair, sixteen inches long. So they said –

Robert's Prosecutor When you were strangling this girl, she reached up and pulled her own *hair*!

Robert (*to Prosecutor*) Hold on.
    (*to audience*) Now when you come up behind me and you strangle me, are you gonna pull your own hair? Or are you gonna pull the hair of whoever back there behind you?

Georgia *Okay?!*

Robert (*to Prosecutor*) You can have a seat.

Robert's Prosecutor sits down.

Robert (*to audience*) And we all knew this white guy, her ex-boyfriend. He had been asking the girl for a date, telling her –

Ex-Boyfriend Why you keep hanging out with all them blacks?

Robert And he asked her that *same night* –

Ex-Boyfriend We gonna go out?

Robert And she said, 'We ain't.'

And so my lawyer, she found out the cops had that hair; she found the guy. He got up and testified at my appeal.

So my lawyer ask him –

Female Lawyer Back in 1990, what color was your hair, and how long was it?

Robert And by then he had short hair, salt-and-pepper, you know, and he said –

Ex-Boyfriend (*on the stand*) My hair was the same color and length back then as it is now.

Robert And my lawyer said –

Female Lawyer Are you sure?

Ex-Boyfriend Of course I'm sure.

Robert So my lawyer pulls out this envelope. And she said –

Female Lawyer Again in 1990, do you remember having your picture taken near the racetrack?

Ex-Boyfriend Uh, yeah.

Robert And then she pulled that big ol' photograph picture out and showed it to him. And there he was, his hair red and brown and sixteen inches long on the picture.

Robert looks to Georgia.

Robert *and* **Georgia** *Okay?!*

Lights down on Robert, Georgia, Ex-Boyfriend, Prosecutor, and Female Lawyer, up on Kerry.

Kerry So then after I've been on death row for twenty-two years, they find this DNA evidence, you know, and the prosecution says that this will be the final nail in Kerry Max Cook's coffin: 'We'll show the world once and for all that he committed that murder.' And then the results come in and it did just the opposite; it finally took the nail out of my coffin, told the world the truth – that that was Professor Whitfield's DNA they found on that girl. And he's still out. They never even went after him. He's been walking around a free man, laughing at the system for twenty-two years.

Twenty-two years.

Lights down on Kerry, up on Gary.

Gary About halfway through my time on death row, a lawyer named Larry Marshall took on my case. He's at Northwestern; he works with a bunch of law students on wrongful convictions. My twin sister found out about him and went down there literally through a blinding snowstorm to see if he would take me on. And he said yes.

Man, that was like the cavalry coming.

Once he started working on it, Larry found out about this motorcycle gang called the Outlaws. Guys gained entrance into the gang by performing violent acts. They killed a bunch of people, they bombed the Hell's Angels – they just did a lot of stuff. And the federal government, the ATF, was running wiretaps on them. Well, in 1995, the ATF got a videotaped confession from an Outlaw guy saying he killed my parents. But I wasn't released until 1996. And that whole year in between, they were fighting my appeal. They fought it all the way to the Illinois Supreme Court.

The two guys who killed my parents were just found guilty last year.

But I've been adamant that those guys not get the death penalty. Some people think that's stupid, but why would I want them to die? It's not gonna bring my parents back. No good's gonna come from it.

Lights down on Gary; up on Sunny and Rhodes.

Sunny (*to audience*) In 1979, Walter Rhodes wrote the following letter to the authorities.

Rhodes I, Walter Norman Rhodes, hereby depose and say that I am under no duress nor coercion to execute this affidavit. This statement is made freely and voluntarily, and to purge myself before my Creator.

Briefly. On February 20, 1976, at approximately 7:15 a.m., I did, in fact, shoot to death two law-enforcement officers with a nine-millimeter Browning pistol.

I state emphatically and unequivocally that my previous testimony against Jesse Tafero and Sonia Jacobs was *false* and part of the statements I was instructed to make by the assistant state attorney, who did coerce me into lying.

I took a polygraph examination relative to this case, but owing to the fact that I am a student of Yoga and karate, and have been for the last ten years, I passed it. And can pass any such test, in my opinion.

The foregoing statements are true and correct to the best of my knowledge and belief. I so swear.

Walter Norman Rhodes, Jr., 9 November 1979.

Lights down on Rhodes.

Sunny Keep in mind that I wasn't released until 1992.

So I'll just give you a moment to reflect: from 1976 to 1992, just remove that entire chunk from your life, and that's what happened.

Long pause, the length of a count of six.

But after all that, one day, the guard came into my cell and told me I was getting out. I thought he was trying to trick me.

Sound of cell door opening. Sunny takes it in.

Sunny And it was just so *joyous*. I mean, I know a lot of people are angry, and I was angry some, but I didn't want to waste my time being mad.

At first, I did everything that Jesse and I said we were going to do together. I went to New York City, I went to the bookstore we said we were going to go to. I bought the book we said we were going to buy to make our Japanese gardens. I was doing it all for both of us.

Lights down on Sunny, up on Delbert.

Delbert When I first got out, I was numb. I didn't sleep for the first three days. I couldn't. And on death row, I had slept like a baby every night.

My first day home, they threw a party at my brother's house. My brother. He gave me his bed for the night – you know, with a red velvet coverlet on it and everything. And one of the sisters from the Defense Committee, she spent the night with me – which was nice, you know.

But I just couldn't get the fuck to sleep, man, and I guess around the third night, I began hallucinating, and one of my friends said, 'Let me call my pastor and ask him to pray for you.' And I talked to the pastor, and he said some kind of prayer and I laid down and went straight to sleep. I haven't had any problems sleeping since then.

After that, the main adjustment was just learning to feel again. You know, when you're in prison, you can't allow yourself to feel too much. So when you get out, you've gotta practice. I had to practice a bunch to be human again. To remind me.

Lights down on Delbert, up on David.

David Maybe I'm still in there, in a way. 'Cause after I was out, I would go to work, I would come home, I would shut the door, and I would lock it. Just like in prison. Go to work, go to the store, come home, lock the door, *click*. Then one day I saw. 'What're you doing lockin' the door?' I say. 'Don't you know you're free now? You're not in lockup any more, man – you're free!'

Prison took away that – spark for life, okay, 'cause in my old pictures from high school, I can see in my face – I'm smilin', you know. And now that's somethin' people round here don't see me do too much, smile.

Sound of rain. David looks up, acknowledges the rain halfheartedly.

In the name of J –

Rain does not stop. Another half try.

In the name of Jesus –

Rain does not stop. David gives up trying. Rain continues softly during the following and slowly fades.

Prison really did somethin' to me.

And now, I do a lot of things – like I may drink, okay, and I smoke some marijuana – to cocaine, to crack cocaine. A perfect day, to me, would be just to get plastered, you know, to forget. 'Cause now I'm tryin' to find out who I am, and if I smoke a joint of reefer, it takes me to that point where I can sit down and write me some poetry or whatever, just like I useta do.

But what are you gonna do? I mean, if they're in power and you have no power, then you're through. Bein' little is like bein' up next to a large oak tree and you just a little small pine. (*Beat.*) That's why, like I said, I really gotta get back into a spirituality thing and focus on findin' that light within . . .'cause that's all I really got, you know.

Lights down on David, up on Kerry and Sandra.

Sandra Actually, I am not a bleeding-heart liberal at all; as a matter of fact, I had a family member murdered and I was always a believer in the death penalty –

Kerry She's a scientist –

Sandra But I was on the board of directors at the Dallas Peace Center and a guy from Amnesty approached me one day and told me he wanted me to help Kerry get integrated into society.

So we were supposed to meet at this conference, and this *boy* walks in. I mean, he had on some jeans and any piece of clothing that had a zipper – you know, from the seventies – it had to have a zipper or he didn't want it. He had grown his hair out and he dyed it – because, you know, he's really nineteen at heart . . . He couldn't look at anyone; he looked down, his leg was shaking the whole time.

Kerry Especially with a female, man, I was supertraumatized about that. Very shy.

Sandra He got up and used the bathroom probably about twenty times because he was so nervous –

Kerry Aw, man, don't tell 'em that –

Sandra But then I thought – and I'm ashamed to have had this thought – what did he do to get himself in that situation? That's how I looked at it . . . 'cause you know, I was very conservative . . . (*Beat.*) and also very stupid. But he gave me the evidence, the hard-core evidence, and it dawned on me, Oh my God, how could this have happened? And he would get so close to you, and then look down . . . and I thought, My God, what has been done to this man?

Kerry The state of Texas executed me over a thousand times, man, and it just keeps on doin' it. I get nightmares – sometimes I forget I'm really here. And every day when I get in the shower, I'm reminded of it, 'cause I cannot avoid the scars all over my body. This is the only woman I've been with since I've been free, 'cause of that, and I married her. Think I'm gonna keep her.

But I'll be honest with you: the price of being here, alive, in this room, is really extraordinary – because when I'm alone, man, especially at night . . . (*Beat.*) Talk about a mental trip, huh?

Lights down on Kerry and Sandra; lights up on Robert and Georgia.

Robert I been out now, three and a half years goin' on four. And we got married, what?

Georgia (*proud*) Two years, 'bout two years –

Robert And she be wanting me to come home, you know at night, and I don't want to come home, I wanna stay out, you know, 'cause if I come home, (*joking*) it makes me feel like I *still locked up*.

Georgia responds.

And you know, there's a lotta times when she go to the store, and she had to knock on the door to let me know she coming in.

Georgia Yeah, he jumps! When I first moved in, I just be walking in, walking out, and he just jump up, 'cause he's just in that mode! I'm like, Okay, he has to take a minute to calm down 'cause he's just used to that. You know, stuff like that plays with your mind.

Robert Yeah, I was in there seven and a half years and it ain't ever gonna go away, far as I'm concerned. Lost my relaxation. Lotta other things, too. You know, you can't really put your thoughts on what you could have lost, or what you *have* lost. I said I could have been a millionaire, or I could have been the police chief. I could have been one of the famous black horse trainers –

Georgia And they won't even give him his license back.

Robert The Trotting Association, they wouldn't even give me my racing license back.

Georgia Can you believe that?

Robert I went to the county; I passed my test with flying colors. They asked me have I ever been convicted of a crime. I put down on the application no, because the Supreme Court, they overturned it. Well, they wrote me back and told me I lied.

Georgia Tell 'em what you told your cousin.

Robert So I told my cousin, I said, 'Well, watch. I can go to a gun shop around here. I'm gonna see if they're gonna deny me. I went and got the gun. But the Racing Commission wouldn't give me my license back. I can legally get a gun, but I can't get a license to drive a horse.

Georgia He can't do something he *likes* to do.

Robert Can't do something I like to do.
   And you know, all I want is, I would like to have me this woman here, a nice piece of land in the country, a nice barn, tractor and a couple of horses. I don't ask for much. But they sayin' I can't. (*Small beat.*) Because of their mistake.

   Lights down on Robert and Georgia, up on Gary and Sue.

Gary What's the matter?

Sue (*to Gary*) I had an incident at the market today, and, and I don't know why it upset me so much, but it really upset me. Some – well –
   Well, it was awful. It was – it was about you.

Gary What, at the market? Somebody didn't like the produce?

Sue No . . . (*to audience*) I mean, this has been over three years now, and this guy was like, you know – (*to Gary*) It started out he just wanted to buy beets. Said –

Lights up on Farmer.

Farmer I want a bushel of beets.

Sue And I told him – (*to Farmer*) 'Well, all of our produce is certified organic.'
And he says –

Farmer Oh, you grew all of this just in water?

Sue I'm like – (*to Farmer*) 'No, that's hydroponic.'
And he asks me –

Farmer Where do you farm?

Sue And I told him. So he said –

Farmer *Oh*, so you farm with that guy that was in all that trouble.

Sue Oh, you mean Gary? Yeah, he's my husband.

Farmer Yeah, that was sort of a fishy case, wasn't it?

Sue Well, you know, two bikers just confessed and were convicted.

Farmer Well, Gauger confessed, too. You know, the paper *said*.

Lights down on Farmer.

Gary (*to Sue*) There's gonna be idiots. I mean, that guy, you know, he's living a lie, just like the newspapers or the prosecutors or whatever. Everyone perceives things in their own way, so which one is the reality, you know? Is the reality your perception? Or is it a composite of everybody's perception, or what?
(*to audience*) I mean, what is reality? We're all light beams, you know –

Sue Oh, Gary, don't go there –

Gary We're all light beams. People wonder, How could God create miracles? Well, because God moves at the speed of light, and time stops, you see. Once you get to the speed of light, you got all the time in the world to change things and create miracles.

Sue (*bemused*) Oh, so you're an expert now?

Gary It's all there on a molecular level, you know. Once somebody told me God is DNA, and you look how tenacious that stuff is you start to wonder.

Lights down on Gary and Sue, up on Sunny.

Sunny You see, I got another chance, because I looked for it. I looked to turn a pile of manure into flowers. I didn't even get lemons; I got manure (*Laughs.*)

I mean, I'm not glad for what happened to me – when I was in there, my parents died, my children grew up without a family . . . and my husband was executed – very, very brutally. Jesse's execution was known worldwide. The chair malfunctioned and made a mess of it. And . . . they had to pull the switch three times.

And he didn't die. It took *thirteen and a half* minutes for Jesse to die. Three jolts of electricity that lasted fifty-five seconds each. Almost a minute. *Each*. Until finally flames shot out from his head, and smoke came from his ears, and the people that came to see the execution, on behalf of the press, are still writing about it. *Ten years afterwards.*

Why do we do that?

Lights down on Sunny, up on Delbert.

Delbert Mahatma Gandhi said that once he discovered who God was, all fears left him regarding the rest of the world, you know, and it's *true*, you know. If you're not harboring any kind of malice, any kind of stuff like that in your heart, there really ain't too much to be afraid of.

And I understand why people are afraid. I mean, I do think the world itself, if you think about it, can be quite frightening . . . I mean just like getting up every day, you know, I understand.

But you can't give in to that. 'Cause as they say in the cowboy pictures, nobody's gonna live for ever, you know what I'm sayin'? And if you have to go, then you might as well go being about the highest thing that you can be about. And that means learning not to fear other people, man, on a *human* level, white or black or *whatever*.

I mean, it's a real struggle not to lump all white people – you know, if you're locked up in a room and a guy comes in wearin' a gray suit and he hits you every time he walks into the room, afterwards you gonna have a thing about people with gray suits, I don't give a fuck who they are.

But I try not to look at the world monolithically like that, and that's what has helped me to survive. I mean, I think the American criminal justice system is totally fucked up – I think some things about our *country* are fucked up – but I also think it's a great country, you know, I really do.

But I mean, the fact that you can have people who probably knew that a lotta folks were innocent – but *they* were not gonna be the ones to lose their jobs, jeopardize their kids' college education, blow their new SUV or whatever for some abstraction like justice. (*Beat.*) That's fucked up.

And I know America gets tired of all of these people talking about what they don't have and what's wrong with the country. Folks say, 'Well what's right with the country?' Well, what the fuck? To make things *better*, we ain't interested in what's *right* with it; we're interested in what's *wrong* with it. You don't say, 'What's *right* with my car?' What's *wrong* with it is what we better deal with.

Lights up on Sunny.

Sunny I want to be a living memorial. When I die, I want
'em to plant tomatoes on me, or apple trees or something,
so that I can still be part of things. And while I'm still
alive, I'm planting my seeds everywhere I go, so that
they'll say, 'I once heard this woman, and she didn't let
them stop her, and she didn't get crushed, and if that little
woman person can do it, then I can do it.' And *that's* my
revenge. That's my legacy, and my memorial.

You know, I've never been to Jesse's grave, and for a
long time it was a bone of contention between his mother
and me. But I explained to her, I said, 'That grave is not
where Jesse really is.' I said, 'That grave is your monument,
and this is mine. My life is my monument.'

Delbert This
     is the place for thoughts that do not end in
          concreteness.
     It is necessary to be curious,
     and dangerous to dwell here; to wonder why
     and how and when is dangerous –
     but *that's* how we get out of his hole.
     It is not easy to be a poet here.
     Yet I sing.
     We sing.

Sound of rain slowly fades in.

(*to David, who does not see him. Lights glow on David*)
Sing.

     *David raises his hand to stop the rain. It does. He
     smiles to himself as Delbert watches. Blackout.*